About the author:
He has two children.

First Published 2011.
Published by Longshot Ventures Ltd, UK.
Printed in the USA.
Copyright Tagore Ramoutar, Longshot Ventures Ltd.

ISBN 978-1-907837-27-2

I Love Vegetables!

Starring Jacob Rabbit

By Tagore Ramoutar

Hello!
My name is Jacob Rabbit.

I am a bouncy rabbit, I like to dance and jump and do karate.

Vegetables are my favourite food! I love them raw and I love them cooked. Come with me to see which of my favourite ones you have tried.

It looks like a tree but tastes great. I like to play races when eating it, to see who can eat it quickest.

This is a field full of cabbages. They are an amazing colour.

I love cabbages!

Mind you, I love sweet corn even more. These are small sweet corn plants.

Corn on the cob is the best. I love eating it hot and nibbling the corn off the cob.

When it gets hot I like to eat salad. Especially green leaves and radishes. Radishes grow underground and are really crunchy.

Aubergines have lovely purple skin and creamy white insides.

Americans call them egg-plants.

Aubergines are really a fruit but most people think they are vegetables.

Peppers come in green, red and yellow! They look great chopped up.

Some vegetables are mainly used in recipes to flavour the food.

Onions are great for flavouring food.

Be careful when chopping them, because onions make your eyes water.

Garlic is also used to flavour food, especially Italian food.

Clusters of garlic are called bulbs.

These are leeks, they are from the same family as onions and garlic and are great in soup. They are also one of the symbols of Wales.

These are sugar snap peas. They are lovely raw, they taste really sweet and crunchy. They are a great treat!

These are runner beans. Before the beans grow there are lovely red flowers.

Do you know potatoes grow in the ground in roots of the plant? To get potatoes you need to dig the plant up.

You can eat them many different ways; chips, mash, new potatoes, baked potatoes or even roast potatoes - my favourite.

Pumpkins are ready to eat in the autumn. You often see them at Halloween, when children use them to make lanterns.

First you scrape out the seeds, then get your Mum or Dad to carve a face in it and put a candle inside.

These are parsnips, they are root vegetables (grow underground). They are great winter vegetables and are lovely roasted.

These root vegetables are called beetroot and their juice makes everything pinkie red including your wee.

Carrots are also root vegetables and are usually orange but can be purple, red, yellow and white! Of course I like orange ones the best. You can eat them raw and cooked.

How many different vegetables did Jacob Rabbit show you?

How many of these have you tasted?

THE END
Other books in the series include
"I Love Fruit! Starring Brownie the Monkey".

www.ingramcontent.com/pod-product-compliance
Lightning Source LLC
Chambersburg PA
CBHW042126040426
42450CB00002B/82